SELECTED POEMS

BOOKS BY BARBARA GUEST

The Location of Things (Tibor de Nagy, 1960)
Poems: The Location of Things; Archaics;
The Open Skies (Doubleday & Company, 1962)
The Blue Stairs (Corinth Books, 1968)
Moscow Mansions (Viking, 1973)
The Countess from Minneapolis (Burning Deck, 1976)
Seeking Air (fiction) (Black Sparrow, 1977)
The Türler Losses (Montréal: Mansfield Book Mart, 1979)
Biography (Burning Deck, 1980)
Quilts (Vehicle Edition, 1981)
Herself Defined: The Poet H.D. and Her World (biography)
(Doubleday & Company, 1984)
Fair Realism (Sun & Moon Press, 1989)
Defensive Rapture (Sun & Moon Press, 1993)

COLLABORATIONS WITH ARTISTS
Musicality (Kelsey Street Press), with June Felter
I Ching (Mourlot Publishers), with Sheila Isham
The Altos (Hank Hine Press), with Richard Tuttle
The Nude (International Editions), with Warren Brandt
Stripped Tales (Kelsey St. Press), with Anne Dunn

Barbara Guest

SELECTED
POEMS

*   *
*

LOS ANGELES
SUN & MOON PRESS
1995

Sun & Moon Press
A Program of The Contemporary Arts Educational Project, Inc.
a nonprofit corporation
6026 Wilshire Boulevard, Los Angeles, California 90036

This edition first published in 1995 by Sun & Moon Press
10 9 8 7 6 5 4 3 2
FIRST AMERICAN EDITION

This book was made possible, in part, through an operational grant from the
Andrew W. Mellon Foundation and through contributions to
The Contemporary Arts Educational Project, Inc.,
a nonprofit corporation

Cover: *Ninth Street, New York* by Barbara Guest
Cover Design: Katie Messborn
Typography: Guy Bennett

LIBRARY OF CONGRESS CATALOGING IN PUBLICATION DATA
Guest, Barbara [1920]
[Poems. Selections]
Selected Poems / Barbara Guest
p. cm.
ISBN: 1-55713-200-3
I. Title.
PS3513.U44A6 1995
811'.54—dc20
95-9742
CIP

Printed in the United States of America on acid-free paper.

To My Daughter

Contents

from POEMS

THE LOCATION OF THINGS

ARCHAICS   THE OPEN SKIES

Belgravia

I am in love with a man
Who is more fond of his own house
Than many interiors which are, of course, less unique,
But more constructed to the usual sensibility,
Yet unlike those rooms in which he lives
Cannot be filled with crystal objects.

There are embroidered chairs
Made in Berlin to look like cane, very round
And light which do not break, but bend
Ever so slightly, and rock at twilight as the cradle
Rocks itself if given a slight push and a small
Tune can he heard when several of the branches creak.

Many rooms are in his house
And they can all be used for exercise.
There are mileposts cut into the marble,
A block, ten blocks, a mile
For the one who walks here always thinking,
Who finds a meaning at the end of a mile
And wishes to entomb his discoveries.

I am in love with a man
Who knows himself better than my youth,
My experience or my ability
Trained now to reflect his face
As rims reflect their glasses,

Or as mirrors, filigreed as several European
Capitals have regarded their past
Of which he is the living representative,
Who alone is nervous with history.

I am in love with a man
In this open house of windows,
Locks and balconies,
This man who reflects and considers
The brokenhearted bears who tumble in the leaves.

In the garden which thus has escaped all intruders
There when benches are placed
Side by side, watching separate entrances,
As one might plan an audience
That cannot refrain from turning ever so little
In other directions and witnessing
The completion of itself as seen from all sides,

I am in love with him
Who only among the invited hastens my speech.

On the Way to Dumbarton Oaks

The air! The colonial air! The walls, the brick,
this November thunder! The clouds Atlanticking,
Canadianing, Alaska snowclouds,
tunnel and sleigh, urban and mountain routes!

     Chinese tree
your black branches and your three yellow leaves
with you I traffick. My three
yellow notes, my three yellow stanzas,
my three precisenesses
of head and body and tail joined
carrying my scroll, my tree drawing

     This winter day I'm
a compleat travel agency with my Australian
aborigine sights, my moccasin feet padding
into museums where I'll betray all my vast
journeying sensibility in a tear dropped before
"The Treasure of Petersburg"

     and gorgeous this forever
I've a raft of you left over
like so many gold flowers and so many white
and the stems! the stems I have left!

Parachutes, My Love, Could Carry Us Higher

I just said I didn't know
And now you are holding me
In your arms,
How kind.
Parachutes, my love, could carry us higher.
Yet around the net I am floating
Pink and pale blue fish are caught in it,
They are beautiful,
But they are not good for eating.
Parachutes, my love, could carry us higher
Than this mid-air in which we tremble,
Having exercised our arms in swimming,
Now the suspension, you say,
Is exquisite. I do not know.
There is coral below the surface,
There is sand, and berries
Like pomegranates grow.
This wide net, I am treading water
Near it, bubbles are rising and salt
Drying on my lashes, yet I am no nearer
Air than water. I am closer to you
Than land and I am in a stranger ocean
Than I wished.

Safe Flights

To no longer like the taste of whisky
This is saying also no to you who are
A goldfinch in the breeze,
To no longer wish winter to have explanations
To lace your shoes in the snow
With no need to remember,
To no longer pull the two blankets
Over your shoulders, to no longer feel the cold,
To no longer pretend in the flower
There is a secret, or in the earth a tomb,
And no longer water on stone hurting the ear,
Making those five noises of thunder
And you tremble no longer.
To no longer travel over mountains,
Over small farms
No longer the weather changing and the atmosphere
Causing delicate breaks where the nerves confuse,
To no longer have your name shouted
And your birthmark again described,
To no longer fear where the rapids break
A miniature rock under your canoe,
To no longer repeat the mirror is water,
The house is a burden to the weak cyclone,
You are under a tent where promises perform
And the ring you grasp as an aerialist
Glides, no longer.

Windy Afternoon

Through the wood
on his motorcycle piercing
the hawk, the jay
the blue-coated policeman

Woods, barren woods,
as this typewriter without an object
or the words that from you
fall soundless

The sun lowering
and the bags of paper
on the stoney ledge
near the waterfall

Voices down the roadway
and leaves falling over there
a great vacancy
a huge left over

The quality of the day
that has its size in the North
and in the South
a low sighing that of wings

Describe that nude, audacious line
most lofty, practiced street
you are no longer thirsty
turn or go straight.

History

for Frank O'Hara

Old Thing

    We have escaped
    from that pale refrigerator

       you wrote about

Here

    amid the wild woodbine landscapes
    wearing a paper hat

I recollect

    the idols
    in those frozen tubs

       secluded by buttresses

when the Church of

       Our Lady cried Enough

and we were banished

Sighing

    strangers
    we are

the last even breath

    poets

Yet the funicular
was tied by a rope

    It could only cry
    looking down

        that midnight hill

My lights are
    bright
the walk is
    irregular

    your initials
    are carved on the sill.

Mon Ami!

    the funicular
    has a knife

        in its side
Ah allow these nightingales to nurse us

Green Awnings

Leander walked over with a basket of peonies.
He was eating grapes he had picked by the old
cottage where he stayed and where there was a door
hung with vines. He was living on grapes, training
his muscles for that solitary climb. Somedays the tower
seemed higher and he felt a little blue twinge
in his arm.

She was sewing a white heron into her gown.
Messages came each day from her father, but
she ignored them, preferring to think of the pale
autumn legs of her bird.

She put water in a vase and wished for flowers.

It was half-past three, but the Latin sun
stayed in the room. How she longed to bathe
in the river. How piteous to be a prisoner
when one was as young as she knew herself to be
in her mirror. She was as earnest as her parents
and nightly prepared her body. She was hopeful
and prayed to the stars who liked her.

She went to the window.

Games need companions, he decided, and sat on the grass.
He had pretended that tree was the armor of his friend, Catylus,
and used up his arrows. The river urged him
to practice his stroke. Later floating on his back,
looking up at the tower, he saw an arm pulling
at an awning strap. What was his surprise when
the green canvas loosed, a girl's hair fell after it.

Santa Fe Trail

I go separately
The sweet knees of oxen have pressed a path for me
ghosts with ingots have burned their bare hands
it is the dungaree darkness with China stitched
where the westerly winds
and the traveler's checks
the evensong of salesmen
the glistening paraphernalia of twin suitcases
where no one speaks English.
I go separately
It is the wind, the rubber wind
when we brush our teeth in the way station
a climate to beard. What forks these roads?
Who clammers o'er the twain?
What murmurs and rustles in the distance
in the white branches where the light is whipped
piercing at the crossing as into the dunes we simmer
and toss ourselves awhile the motor pants like a forest
where owls from their bandaged eyes send messages
to the Indian couple. Peaks have you heard?
I go separately
We have reached the arithmetics, are partially quenched
while it growls and hints in the lost trapper's voice
She is coming toward us like a session of pines
in the wild wooden air where rabbits are frozen,
O mother of lakes and glaciers, save us gamblers
whose wagon is perilously rapt.

Dardanella

Those forms in gauze
     we see as arches
the tile replaces with mountain
the script says: As water this life
poets go to the mountain
followed by girls in white

The king of the heavy mustache
"like buffaloes these men"
cannot find dawn in his sleep

So agents prepare the morning mosquito
it must be noisy yet not alarming

Those who hear it across the valley
in their ears closed with honey
will feel the sting of bells

in the palace only one vase need splinter

from his arms only the virgin need struggle

the boy knows now to kiss

he will ride horses to the blue dome.

Twenty-four veils in a pile
and hatchoutchoui houri
for hours and hours and hours
the patient needy camel lifts his neck
over the sun brick petals catch
that is all…no vines…no miles
…no hills…no caves in the hills…

women walk to the fountain

Pasha is with the Consul
the French woman writes letters a violet eye

toward the boy who has peed on the tile
she forgets the name for raisin says plum

Milk say the heavens regarding the white sand

Bosphorus click of eel in your wave off Egypt
tow-ridden plain of Kilid Bahr
trees and risk where ancient bouncing flat
is war land of the tomb otherwise lids

Air in the arch is black
as sighs from vessels cast
on the shut-off tide.

Sand

The distance
     see
the miles produce
     reckoning,
water
     extending
Sand
     while
the sky airs itself
     requests
clouds remain
     in numbers
far off
also
     the hand,
eyes, limbs
sand tests
     coolness and heat
     body levels

     …Remain flat
planes fly over you
under a belly
     prone side
of earth end

     Neutral
to haughty black land and sea
     that swank of blue
clammering
     greed of ear
and rapacious its thunder,

or even the mild wave at
dawn's edge
     a honey
when youthfully it begins to boil
and foam wildly spilled
     ...noonday

     Salt throat
the tongue clasps the swell,
releases sends monitoring ceaseless
thirst back to ocean depth
        tides return to dark

     The skeleton
shock of wave lift, a column
on the shore its profile ever foreign
its ruin permanent   recurs

The bowl has changed color
gulls flown inland,
Poets walk across you their footprints
cannot shock your softness, on you
shells, pearls, weeds
discards as on a mountain top
is found record of horizon

as Patmos is an isle,

As you are mouth and sable skin
range of the sandle-footed

Rejoice
in ancient nothingness

from THE BLUE STAIRS

Fan Poems

I

Who walks softly causes mutiny among the lilies
as a chateau is perverse refusing wings,
refusing a colder climate for its rooms;
and the blossoms fall repeatedly, exciting
those unique flower beds when at morning's edge
they hasten to lift themselves to a cautious heel print.

II

Windows, Melissa, they contain what is best
of us, the glass your arm has arranged
into crystal by spinning eye, by alarms
taken when the rain has chosen a form
unlike the universe, similar to ups and downs
which vary or change as cowslips
in the meadow we cross have a natural tint,
the panes reflect our hesitations and delight.

III

Repeatedly striking, i.e., to strike the imagination
another blow, neither heat nor cold,
but the power in the wing, the chill

smothering feather outlined narrowly
by vertebrae extended for an instant;
it makes one shudder, the quick umbrella
unfurled near the tearful statue.

IV

Traditional service to and from
like elastic. It covers ten moments
and maybe twenty. The wound is safely
succored, the branch spared from storm.
I have covered a hundred miles on vibrating
tires, they hum a safe tree.
The highway oaks are undisturbed
their age protects adventure, giving
visual shelter encouraging voices
to clear themselves from stanza to mute stanza.

V

Classically perchance am I your robin
or rossignol, not hirondelle, that dark
word ending in dress? At the top of stairs
stands the Marquis wearing a burnt
ribbon, wearing an 'air,' so they say,
I wonder at its quaintness, I wonder also
at my hoops, my stays are 'pinching,'
let us take the night air in an ice.

VI

Why not make a perspective of ancient allée
so that it can promenade? You'd probably
end with muslin, catching the lion's curve
as he backs into pond, seconds before the wet tail lashes;
As this hour presents us with what it knows best,
as this hour wishes to retire rather than wander.

VII

What I recall of your romance
is: "sleep is milk."
Saluting the gypsies and always thirsty.

A Reason

That is why I am here
not among the ibises. Why
the permanent city parasol
covers even me.

It was the rains
in the occult season. It was the snows
on the lower slopes. It was water
and cold in my mouth.

A lack of shoes
on what appeared to be cobbles
which were still antique

Well wild wild whatever
in wild more silent blue

the vase grips the stems
petals fall   the chrysanthemum darkens

Sometimes this mustard feeling
clutches me also. My sleep is reckoned
in straws

Yet I wake up
and am followed into the street.

A Way of Being

There we go in cars, did you guess we wore sandals?
Carrying the till, memorizing its numbers,
apt at the essential such as rearranging
languages. They occur from route to route
like savages who wear shells.

"I cannot place him." Yet I do.
He must ascend indefinitely as airs
he must regard his image as plastic,
adhering to the easeful carpet that needs
footprints and cares for them
as is their wont in houses, the ones we pass by.

Such a day/or such a night
reeling from cabin to cabin
looking at the cakewalk or merely dancing.
These adventures in broad/or slim
lamplight,

                        Yet the cars
do not cheat, even their colors perform in storm.
We never feel the scratch, they do.
When lightning strikes it's safer to ride
on rubber going down a mountain,
safer than trees, or sand, more preventive
to be hid in a cloud we sing, remembering

The old manse and robins. One tear,
a salty one knowing we have escaped
the charm of being native. Even as your glance
through the windshield tells me you've seen
another mishap of nature

you would willingly forget,
prefer to be like him near the hearth
where woodsmoke makes a screen of numbers and signs
where the bedstead it's not so foreign as this lake.

The plateau, excursionist,
is ahead. After that twenty volumes
of farmland. Then I must guide us
to the wood garage someone has whitened
where the light enters through one window
like a novel. You must peer at it
without weakening, without feeling
hero, or heroine,

Understanding the distances
between characters, their wakeful
or sleep searchingness, as far from the twilight ring
the slow sunset, the quick dark.

Parade's End

The most that can be said
for following the parade
is that the Head was red.

Liking grotesque the architect
went along with it,
the balloons and the bellies
enlarged.

He had a craze for size,
so he said.

Looking at it from the sidelines
we weren't so amused
as chilled by the snow wind,
our feet getting smaller
in unadaptable leather

our eyes formed truly gigantic tears

we dropped when the last
soldier had passed and the confetti
was buried in the ash can.

It was quite a day. I brought home
an unopened poem. It should grow
in the kitchen near the stove
if I can squeeze out of my eyes
enough water. Water.

Saving Tallow

Visible tallow of the hurricane night
thin fair candle
a yacht cradling
the room's deep water

                  where the wave
raises

                  its sail
a procession

                  of shoulders
the falling olives

                  on yellow knees
and cities

                  drowned
in their comet clothing

                  dragged from the sea

                  Candle!
lone palm tree   lonely diver
covered with sea lice

                  most vertical
the room dedicates its curves to you.

                  There was once a shadow
called Luis; there was once an eyebrow
whose name was Domingo. Once there
were children, grown-ups, organs;
there were moving legs and there was
speech. In the daylight there were

small whimpers made by the African cat;
in the candlelight there were couplings
of such sonority evening callers
merely left their cards; no one drew back
the curtains; there were no curtains
the candlelight fell on grass and
like a candle up stood the water hose.

                There were many mathematical
forms
                the obliquity of a painting
                her mouth drawn by a corner
transverses on the arrow light
                where the smile flies off
at the room's center a hair part
                the nose of a window
                louvered as coral rock
                where a person walked

                was sleepy
                must be awakened
for adorations and questions

                is marine
related to the diving fish

                Take me on your dolphin skin!
                I shall be absent soon!

Saving the tallow with capable hands
seizing with the loyal closed eyes of foliage

                Puff

Walking Buddha

Should I forget your scales
in confirmation of your knighthood

        or voice what is petal-soft
        in the cracked eye-lift?

Not circular or fleeting
but *swinging*

        pushed forward by your idiom
        like a giantess opening a window sash

you refuse to remark
the offering below your building

        you refuse to go downstairs
        because your gait is forward
        we must go around you

Brilliant decision!

        a frangipane rewards you
        with color streak

in the wet season

        that coloring protects

better than ghee, better than opium

A metal eye that cannot open

stretched as far as elephant, yet firm
in its enclosure

Diadem head!

The masons have finished their research

not a cubic inch more

There is:

The arm whose elongation

the open hand the chest measurements

Rough cement ruled

an original of ART BRUT

unrailed staircase

a smash knee surface

to conceal the bronze asperity

essentials of being classical
in a violent world before the decline

under slip-shoe palm

A Handbook of Surfing

I

It is time to find the peak the rosy trimmings are sliding up

toward you whose fingers reach over the balcony the flowers

and trees are damp morning up breaks differently each sibilant

wavering the night closet shut   seeks…

A circular moon continued; ideal these conditions a
settled air on its five or six feet the wave rocks
early over the coast foam line spews as once at her lightest
the goddess washed goats tumbled into the brine mark their forks
body erect and facing the shore margin he of the water sign
    considers

…Bottom what is there under the shell determining size and
    type
those coral rocks an idiot glance from crevice to crevice they
    watch
the smooth wave. Why did Columbus the Navigator
select the reef? Its products are strong even off the simple isle.
Sand bottom more fickle rippling sand roulette, a dusty
depth and shifty, an unknown alphabet whose squeaky
letters as apt to let one down or forget to lift us up, we
cannot always climb the sand horn or blowing
hot then cold erratic it sometimes sleeps in the dovecote water.

Domestic requisites (agricultural, manufactured, urban,
                    non-urban, marital or no)
have placed you here sun-struck and geared
with your ocean plan for a soupy ride
right or downside
eyewash of roar speech saltness he thinks less thus
is better to concentrate the hash of whether/or

                    …No one has gentled this leash
                    Not you marbled H's

In the wave wilderness wily wild
cuckoo strength bearers as rapists
knee songs and thigh grippers
foam slashers bone knockers
surf kindlers in the riddle splash
                    t   wit   ter   woo
like a long legend

                    II

Since there are probably no two surfers in the world who
will agree one hundred percent on the techniques of
advanced surfing, we would like to deal only with
the basic principles of learning to surf…we would
like to tell here about paddling, standing and turning,
straightening out or pulling out, we shall discuss
the effect of tides and bottom conditions…

Paddling is prone or kneeling or sitting
Standing and Turning mean exactly that plus some wisdom
as when you go down a hill on your heels and up one
on your toes. Everyone knows how to turn or turn about

or make a reverse these are daily decisions both
politic and poetic and they have historic sequences
in the surf they are known as Changing Directions

as is seen a darting fish

yet we deserve reunion

it soothes

this peak mounting even in ruffled calm
to search this way and that on the desert a palm
a white car to guide swiftly
as quoted my paddling self you have veins in your hands

Ardent days! Golden backs! The pier
at your peak helmeted one   hot dogging
the shore break   well there are many types of
waves they all fall (differently) you must assume
the General Positions:

on nose
spinning
driving down
head dips

Duke Kahanamoku

Makaha

Excellencies on the woodless sands

your emblem of polyurethane

Today I shall walk the board my teak sandals
on the wax the surf's down waterwheel furled
the monkey figure of moustached shiverless scale
we are also goons with our bent backs
not so turbulent in the shallows, but boring
as after prayers and feasting the sleepy travellers

III

Paddling out: Tributes must be paid that this
waterway be freed

and further: I think I see you blink in Iceland
top pole of wave
your midnight eye at crest   there
Viking foam…barriers the pine seed

Rolling through: On the way to line up it's under the soup
you with your immaculate verb sense the
indicative clause so under control and
the novel how much you understand of
character plot action not to
mention vice or the splitting sensitivity of
Balzacian Frabrizio and those days in
so long Trevio   I remark your courage when
you decide the form is exactly at its crest of
sequence as in England the forty long spins
take us to India and back or within
a wearisome reach so tiring this spin on
top of water   Now roll your board under
you go the big spume breaks you're safe
with your underwater cartilage it's only
a quaint mishap to be thrown by imagination

and never if you're careful. While you wait
the longest while the first chapter, never
fear your head will roll on top. Not even
depth, but spun ivy tickle water
you're up then you're on top. A hard
way to it and the only. Just the beginning
Mister Tom. I mean master of swallows

the dynamite crest

(Where are the childish waves the lappings
eschewed as to the lighthouse balloons
against a window your narrow partings)

IV

Wondering if this day fills you with ennui as it does me
in your bunnyhood so busy on the beach opening tops
six package I'm told. Where is your yellow long
veiled anger where is your passion diphthong?
On the beach with only vulture gulls can you
forget your dislike of bibliothèque?

Go
orange volume sandy named a windy
nomenclature suitable or yours pensioned

Lo your glossy tunics the simple wrap around
or take off always one shoulder the porous
statues on the hill stanced seaward sunstruck
withered frequently headless only the bosoms
upholding strict maidens courageous also

so many storms and tribal wars so much murder
to remain unburied…the warrior torso
over whom you keep watch remembering this beauty
especially at full moon one hand disjointed
severed reaches still to you as on the waveboard

        a girl takes the wing position the surfer's arm
        upholds so at Samothrace so will capture
        Boreas all bunnies the wind speaks finally
        air braided of wind is your upward tether
        not these duplicate days you expend
                …your mosaics
        will they survive the dolphin's flight?

                    v

Questing the oracles en route to wave line-up
what did the breezes sing whisking the vases
the stern crones at idle nine o'clock did they repeat
flat or uncommon sea surf down or up
we'll know soon enough when the obituaries are out
each year another statesman back wash to our policy
our double daring life dips   owl not gull
be wise tell us when the necessary pull out

        this one yonder at its peak if too grand
        bail out you can't get away with everything
        even in your detective clothes sometimes
        as now one can continue the turn a right
        or left motion dependent on guerrilla wave strength

Dashed if I didn't flub it…remember
"All can transform the ugly wipeout
into a thing of beauty"
can save face even in oceanic pratfall
recognizing superior strength takes moral
courage once gained on a really critical turn
later made the pipeline but don't
expect each year to
                cop the Kangaroo crown

You with your lease on World Championship

VI

    Surfari…

        if you travel the water ways
in a moment you find the sluice gates
as if / the shut of a book when
before your eyes you study its rhyme
I call remark the seconds before sunset
when vaporizing the smoke night
        sets its teeth
I'd rather a more vigorous selection
        two stanzas at twilight
        you hear ringing the columns

VII

Hélas! "In closeout conditions no one surfs"
There is a point beyond which big storm surf is unrideable
The four fathom five you hope to squire

sweet gauzy weeds to be coronals
on oceanic floor swaying they've learned their dance
they have a habit of performing without audience;
yet greed, for they are penniless, makes them desire a swimmer.

Am called Cassandra in these summer days
when in the soft illness of heat I'm ready
to talk of battles

>He rides in the heat
>he never squeaks
>he is ready for shore order

whether/or the village cong cough
like a leaky board when the surf is rough
Cassandra thinks of a child whose muscles
are thin; she weeps at the motorboard cost
the reef he'll hit young as Wordsworth's Lucy
in the quick clime of bomb

>Protest!

Nobody rides in closeout!

VIII

In the polyandry green of life there's a rule you stride

>quick to the whip before the foam
>the complexion of green
>shadows under the sandcove eyes
>the slim waistline of coast

to be adored as you glide spookless
this rhythm ancient as self the muslin shore

      with these lenses use nothing more
      all that is not goggle is giggle
      take this most intricate tide
      in your own way knowing the cost
      forsaking all others if need be
      it at its dangerous crest

   mortuary bottom

Gallantly these fine surf horses
(innocently capturing a beach as daylight
finds the old sea at its best cooler
more quiet the dawn strokes
a way to greet heroes   the flat hues
let them rest)
        battle form

we acquiesce

      the purchasable line

promptly renewing our lids/our eyes

to negotiate each splendid day

we do this from wave couch

in shrewdness meditate

the expanse   the artful dare

from MOSCOW MANSIONS

Red Lilies

Someone has remembered to dry the dishes;
they have taken the accident out of the stove.
Afterward lilies for supper; there
the lines in front of the window
are rubbed on the table of stone

The paper flies up
then down as the wind
repeats. repeats its birdsong.

Those arms under the pillow
the burrowing arms they cleave
at night as the tug kneads water
calling themselves branches

The tree is you
the blanket is what warms it
snow erupts from thistle;
the snow pours out of you.

A cold hand on the dishes
placing a saucer inside

her who undressed for supper
gliding that hair to the snow

The pilot light
went out on the stove

The paper folded like a napkin
other wings flew into the stone.

Illyria

And I was right as dawn over head
listening to the buoy as is often done
a bridge while brows float under it yes
it was a way of steeples of construction
of pilings of verbs. I too admire the way
water spells in the hand riding this way and
that and also the moments of green which
like paragraphs point out the stations
we must enter and leaving them count trees
more scarcely; there is much to emulate
not only iron bands but those waves you can
no longer dive into and the seamless rifts
which are noble as you explain omnivorously
having devoured both nail and hammer,
like an isle composed of rhythm and whiteness.
Night is gentle with the promise
of a balanced pear such is it this drop.

Egypt

for Tony Smith

Because nobody knew whether it was Monday or Tuesday
the park that was on Monday began on Tuesday

This water flows either ways with exceptions
for blue moments described as loaded when

Never to make a remark about merely a generous lump
leaves no ivy over your tough Pharaoh meter

Either liked to parade in front of mirrors
going underground was a busy strike so that

When examined the bird's tread went which way
and that the pastime was being amazed

And getting out the size of a hump

The storage space it occupied "simple, very
authoritative, very enduring things."

A vigorous antiquity into which the slab was
inserted and either said not enough in spite of

The ribbons of oozes nobody made an oasis
out of it until dissatisfactions

With sizes more confusing than the tomb
where zero unwraps Ouch! you've printed my thumb

You have lost the original which was perhaps
better but the boys did their best lying on the

Mowed grass whispering butter as a matter of fact

Nebraska

Climate succumbing continuously as water gathered
into foam or Nebraska elevated by ships
withholds what is glorious in its climb like
a waiter balancing a waterglass while the tray
slips that was necklace in the arch of bridge
now the island settles linear its paragraph of tree
vibrates the natural cymbal with its other tongue
strikes an attitude we have drawn there on the limb
when icicle against the sail will darken the wind
eftsooning it and the ways lap with spices as
buoyancy once the galloping area where grain
is rinsed and care requires we choose our walk

And the swift nodding becomes delicate
smoke is also a flow the pastoral calm where
each leaf has a shadow fortuitous as word
with its pine and cone its seedling a curl
like smoke when the ashy retrograding slopes
at the station up or down and musically
a notation as when smoke enters sky

The swift nodding becomes delicate
'lifelike' is pastoral an ambrosia where calm
produces a leaf with a shadow fortuitous as word
with its pine and cone its seedling we saw
yesterday with the natural flow in our hand
thought of as sunlight and wisely found rocks

sand that were orisons there a city in
our minds we called silence and bird droppings
where the staircase ended that was only roof

Hallucinated as Nebraska the swift blue
appears formerly hid when approached now it
chides with a tone the prow striking a grim
atmosphere appealing and intimate as if a verse
were to water somewhere and hues emerge
and distance erased a swan concluding bridge
the sky with her neck possibly brightening
the machinery as a leaf arches through its yellow
syllables so Nebraska's throat

Knight of the Swan

He left the trees when he left the lake
because he was careless with catacombs and fear

He mounted the swan and rode away

Knight of the Swan

Those feathers you press with a heavy intent and
thoughtfulness gathering speed while the reins slip
loosely the muscular bird neck   on past
The Girl Asleep in the Window   then later
The Farmstead Beneath Trees   he smiles the bird
quivers yet sober as bridges in autumn
there is a haze on these miles and the swan needs
water whose body is heated with mountains

They walk in   tattery   rain

A few quick oaths   long space

More lengthening   a gentian

They fly   he has made

(an escape)   the swan is furious

The Knight feeds it some smiles

They lumber on

                                'shadowy evening'

Makes her escape

                    and a garment falls over the swan
an umbrella poem of pale irons and acrobat tones
a confusing reward for sleep instead of that sweet presence
until morning brought the rainbow in different styles rather
than weather; yet they were relieved and hastened on
more enemies now than beast and knight so it seemed
but it was less so they were stumbling together; hidden
under his feathery pants and the swan's heavy down
were landmarks that were similar despite the knight's
peasant past and the swan's poet future

Things that might have been bullets hit his insides
(he was wary) they were not bullets they were adventures
which sting although not lethal and because they often
flew very high what caused his sensation was hyperion
or a bolt from the sun and it was azure which caused
him to sink onto the swan's down it was that bordered
by snow and flower when a quick look would make you dizzy

and below a tidal swamp was dark and lurking strange
faces were lit by fire the heights on which he perched
made them unordinary there were instant foamings out of
the dew where this knight sought a castle he trembled so
he fought with his damp forehead he clutched the swan
for he with his new agony asked the swan if

                         the swan responded
flights are macaroons it almost said being weblike
often lacking a breeze they have an order like my neck

I would like to make love to you said the knight

The swan with an abrupt gesture of its wings set him down
in the forest (nearby) nearby was a lake from whence
they had originated   it was indeed nearby   the knight
began to relax and to breathe to   suspire   he cast

aside those odious thoughts of his origin   he began
(with dreamy asides)   to like wings   there was obviously
too much noise when a wave hit a concave stone   yet here

here in the lightness which repeats itself as darkness
he often returns a wanderer   he stoops for the token

                    the token

            wizened   as an orange tooth
                        becomes an irritant when the wind
            harshens and grass is seamier than old rags
            in the knot of the hurricane   a vase of empty
            rags the healthier shore calls 'refuse' thus
            sends them spinning like nutmegs from the shoots
            that bore them

                    we see signals
            as tokens they burden our clothes when light
            buttons down and sheets are shaken in the dust
            of widening rooms

                    we see where asphodels
            we hunt archways where turtles are strewn
            like wreaths of sofas and rugs (the daffodils)
            and draperies (like hands)   tokens

the statuary and rabbits   the tins   the gasps
going to the theatre   descending
he was seized with a fit of tokens they caught him
pitilessly   joylessly   noblessly an eyeful
the parent company made the toys (a token)
the sibling company sold them
going to your desk in the meadow
finding a token in the drawer…

the drawer
"It seems I can't ever win," he said shaking out the drawer
"Until she appears" then she did appear she did fanning
his wrists like an old timer she had croupier spirit
in every breath she drew like a swimmer who draws the ocean
or a worm who draws the earth or I who draw
your heaviness as you draw the drawer as
daylight draws to its close all have endings
like berries drawn in snow
like brownness that once was berries
drawn in snow

a snow tale

of a foot having a high instep
that was frozen in a storm when somebody
took off its snowshoe

the shoe was only an idea.

Counting 2 lunches and 2 teas we've done rather well.
We haven't lost any snows over it.

the gingerale

was a lesson in how to do nothing if ever he watched one.
The shadowy spot at the top where the shoe used to be
the token   the drawer   the gingerale
                        could be put in a chimney
and out would pour a shadowy spot or so one thinks
yet a purr glistens

                        on the rock
where a tall man sits puffing and he lengthens
his shadow by drinking in sips as one would tease
gingerale by spitting or by reading
the spirit goes out of it and presently there is only
a tall glass a bird sings in the tree near it

                                it

stirs up a little rain
on top of IT

 (it) must
go inside of IT

returning the token was more like a landing commenced in a
                                                moonsoon
the feathery tides nearly drowned it where the lake's waves

  the waves of the lake swelled like mulberries in a damp tin box
whose very grin was icy like particular thoughts of finding
and loss and the difficulties of property on sand

                        in the autumn

rinsing the token and ridding it of dispiritedness a cold
foam bath and icy smiles the lips permitted and the knight
was refreshed then also the mountains had reviving airs

nesting in the hollows from peak to golden peak and there were
lairs for robbers which altered the loneliness

for always he wished for his swan even its shadow even
a shadow on stones that once were heavy and warm

    and the swan's story

he cherished along with the memory of his ride that as a basin
is filled then emptied yet its curve remains and its depth

he would never forget nor the exact three quarter of his waltz
there on the fringes of clouds and the embrace in the chasm

with snow and down erasing any doubt the act was modern

    as mountain climbing or looking for gentians

any ruin has its surplus or wrinkle there on the mask

    fed with dishes of rain

the knight was no exception he even wore his hair like a legend
whistling a lot from a need for quaintness he plied himself
back and forth pretending he had an occupation like speech

     of course it was the same

even the military and the religious wherever there was a crowd
especially at the inn the enjoyment was the same either
more or less creating a contemporary scene against the morass
also the skis were the same with their question of advance
or slumber the echoes were like that multiplying the same

avenues

                                      they were the same as trails
with the heavy youths attacking the scrub the same
as sidewalks in summer like pointed firs the escape
was the same as the cellar door a language of weather

and straw

                  much faded while he slept.

The night animals advanced   the tender snow
roofless and perspicacious the way apples mix with cinders
the animals tore at his coat they reminded him of the chance
he took and what it meant in terms of courage
and the tendency to keep his eyes closed in daylight
he wished the oyster snow would go away
or the paws and he quietly atone for those meadows
employing a different voice he woke himself up
the creatures fled through the trees but the brass struck
harder in a persistent rhythm both alarming
and lulling

                 a cantus firmus

"I must   the most of"
"I must   to the"
"I must polish my armor" is what it added up to

the rest is flurry or a forecast of   the terms
were regular owls returning to their pasture spooky too
unlike a crowded barn the slope with its slight condensing
of timber and snow reflected an austere history   the story

of a family that had passed its days dutifully
(rather like the knight before he met his swan)

Now he shook with glee and oaths   violets thrust themselves
up at him and he seized a handful so a tremor of Spring
passed through him not knowing which way it was meant to go

with the tilt of flowers
with the floral tilt

                          with the wilt of snow
like a building surfaced in stucco
or a white machine crossing a bridge
or air with a cloud woven in that space where
a motor threads it a short black lace thickening
the atmosphere the way a weaver does

so a chivalric mood occupied the knight

                 like a hand.

          Occupied by a chivalric mood

the Knight refuses to disturb the hand

it was the hand

                    opened books and doors for him
that fed and soothed when the long train
crossed his brow stirring the cars above his fears

the hand

                    forbidding encounters even excursions

as winter light interpolates sun

                    what was shiny or angled

cleared/straightened in a tiny slaughter

                    the objects rocking back and forth

unharmed yet like a torrent cut off from
mountain water and somewhat shallow as birds

skimming low were fleshy and bright not so poignant
as the swan in white intentness trial of wings

                    the hand

was a substitute

                    an arch leading into the proscenium

yet
the aspect was bare

      it shivered in short grass

where
possibly ruins or ornaments lay

      breathless.

The Knight preferred the way his swan
      had kicked up its wings
this limp air and that calm hand
      made a classic life
he realized he could get on better
      the way one progresses through green
on a minimal plain

      without exasperations & doubts

he regretted this loss of impetuousness

only gratitude seeped over the thin stream

and his smile placed by the hand

      was sweet

one or two muscles quivered
reminiscence of his flight

      he wished these books

were thornier

                              the doors

noisy

       when he learned their names

              It's raining
              said the Knight
              let's walk.

Roses

"painting has no air…"
—GERTRUDE STEIN

That there should never be air
in a picture surprises me.
It would seem to be only a picture
of a certain kind, a portrait in paper
or glued, somewhere a stickiness
as opposed to a stick-to-it-ness
of another genre. It might be
quite new to do without
that air, or to find oxygen
on the landscape line
like a boat which is an object
or a shoe which never floats
and is stationary.

         Still there
are certain illnesses that require
air, lots of it. And there are nervous
people who cannot manufacture
enough air and must seek
for it when they don't have plants,
in pictures. There is the mysterious
traveling that one does outside
the cube and this takes place
in air.

It is why one develops
an attitude toward roses picked
in the morning air, even roses
without sun shining on them.
The roses of Juan Gris from which
we learn the selflessness of roses
existing perpetually without air,
the lid being down, so to speak,
a 1912 fragrance sifting
to the left corner where we read
"The Marvelous" and escape.

Byron's Signatories

1

His air of the underworld

His air of the underworld…the underleaf
of the catalpa together with the ruddiness
of his lisp.

2

Lately he said you've a shocking
amount of premature histories,
your stockings have runs. It is
the Alaska pipeline all over all
over. In the polar morning that
should be dusk does it matter
                    about gloves?

3

Supposedly more religious
to do it in geometrics, without images
with an acoustical sound,
like 'ees' that are closer
to a childhood of alphabets

The way that it murmured. And
you were here all the while. Sleeplessly
as a diet counts grams those
valves continuing with you
in the distances

They are asymmetrical. Also mountains
with their dark and quiet.

4

shabby sequences as sorrows repeating

or the soft voice of her who found rest
in the rich cracker not wanting to breathe

      with your buttons and marbles
as the day turned with lateness and monuments
        consumed all that
        now it's not a dream

5

           I admire you
in your Byron green suiting clipping away
at a language. And I liked also the fragments;
the bit of sail, the heel of the island,
even the letter going clop clop on its piece
of thread especially that hint about your
half sister and nearly setting a tone

6

Clarice recounted her summer near Lucca
swings and whispers food
at the fountains and the baths
surrounded by marble (Carrara) near
turnstiles yet it was only a week
I mean the vacation meant longer
but politics put them all to bed
on a train the chesty part was reaching
the Alps in a Rover—alas!

7

Yesterday I saw an etching by Hirschvogel
called "Landscape with Two Buildings
Surrounded by Water," such a derivative
title I considered tearing it up it was
really so literal, yet the drawing was
spooky in the German fashion one
kept peering up at windows conjuring
rigid sleeves and hearts plunged
or purged was the intent of the arrows

8

Having a rough moment and indigestion
the rug clung to you George Gordon
even if its repetitions were termed neglect.
A little went a long way
(like bricks on a Turkish oven)
still . . the tent didn't hold in the foam.

9

Living solitarily in the garret reading Strindberg in the afternoon stuffing the window with paper shortening her walks because of the cold…she welcomed his visits. At first they were daily, then hourly, now only minutes would elapse before she heard his rap at the door. His arrival was usually preceded by a twinge on her left retina something like tequila, a rough peppery hotness she called it the 'flavor of eyes.' They would talk together as long as they could. There were various passages he liked to indulge in and she would follow him there rubbing against the wall, avoiding as best she could the damp, but liking the shreds of scenery he invited her into and the hesitations in his vocabulary that were like shrubbery brown at the squat root and silvery green on the charged outsides. And so she was isolated no longer and rather thought of him as her drawbridge similar to the one in the picture by Hirschvogel…

10

Up at the "Mansion"
Davy sat on the bed lighting a cheroot.
Peter talked of Agnes in the arcade.
A thing or two "lifted" there.
People whistling in corridors
riffs from "Ecuador."
You could see the mold
from which the jelly was pressed.

11

But the world changed
leaving us on its lid

    patches, mostly, elsewhere
    a fugue and then the scratch on the arm

More snow floating from Moscow
there on the road; the bandana

    chortling at a few prisoners.

The Poetess

after Miró

A dollop is dolloping
her a scoop is pursuing
flee vain ignots   Ho
coriander darks   thimble blues
red okays adorn her
buzz green circles in flight
or submergence?   Giddy
mishaps of blackness make
stinging clouds what!
a fraught climate
what natural c/o abnormal
loquaciousness   the
Poetess riddled
her asterisk
genial!   as space

The Stragglers

If you lift your arms
against the white door
   'not to fall'

Or if autumn or climate
or the pencil with its skill
   'almost germanic'

a contest where the white will
   that shrinks
in weather…under the moon

   they assemble
the portative number
   the bridge with its figures
the blossoming twelve
   treading ice

those closets of doves. also figurative.
and walking home. on rugs.

from THE COUNTESS FROM MINNEAPOLIS

River Road Studio

Separations begin with placement
that black organizes the ochre
      both earth colors,

Quietly the blanket assumes its shapes
as the grey day loops along leaving
an edge (turned like leaves into something else),

Absolutes simmer as primary colors
and everyone gropes toward black
where it is believed the strength lingers.

I make a sketch from your window
the rain so prominent earlier
now hesitates and retreats,

We find bicycles natural
under this sky composed of notes,

Then ribbons, they make noises
rushing up and down the depots
at the blur exchanging
its web for a highway.

Quartets the quartets
are really bricks and we are
careful to replace them
until they are truly quartets.

Prairie Houses

Unreasonable lenses refract the
sensitive rabbit holes, mole dwellings and snake
climes where twist burrow and sneeze
a native species

into houses

corresponding to hemispheric requests
of flatness

euphemistically, sentimentally
termed prairie.

On the earth exerting a willful pressure

something like a stethoscope against the breast

only permanent.

Selective engineering architectural submissiveness
and rendering of necessity in regard to height,
eschewment of climate exposure, elemental
        understandings,
constructive adjustments to vale and storm

historical reconstruction of early earthworks

and admiration

for later even oriental modelling

for a glimpse of baronial burdening
we see it in the rafters and the staircase heaviness
a surprise yet acting as ballast surely

the heavens strike hard on prairies.

Regard its hard-mouthed houses with their
robust nipples the gossamer hair.

JOHN GRAHAM riding in his coach to meet the Countess stopped at the mansion of Larisnov on Summit Avenue for a sudden glass of tea. The two men strolled in the garden that overlooked the city of St. Paul commenting on the various fixtures and incompletions, the domes, the central plazas and that avid air of chance hanging, as always, over a capitol.

It was in that garden the laws of Minimalism as opposed to Baroque were formed and the great Futuristic statements came about, climaxing in "less is Mores" which led to a general razing of the remnants of the late nineteenth century that in their generous furry way were suffocating the capitol.

"Remember deterioration is embarrassing," added John Graham, (Ivan Dabrosky) and jumped into his carriage to continue on to his rendez-vous with the Countess.

"This street reminds me of scarceness, even loss like searching for hen's teeth in the rain," murmured the Countess to herself as she picked her way slowly down Hennepin Avenue. "I feel frightfully sad somehow and truly lost. I wish I had a glass of sherry right now, only that would never do. I mean I couldn't drink it here on the corner. Look at that gutter. So muddy. The wind's from the Southeast which should mean...I never know what it means. The prairies confuse me so. Perhaps Liv will have a hot bath ready when I finally reach home. That and the new frock from New York with the twin reveres. I wonder how reveres shall look on top of mutton sleeves. There's venison for supper. And the St. Louis Dispatch with luck should have arrived." The Countess hesitated for a moment as the sidewalk drifted into dirt and her grey eyes filled with dust.

Seated at the mirror rolling up her hair, feeling the thin papers curling around her fingers, the air in contrast thick from the low glaucous clouds, the color of flour, her fingers twisting the papers into shapes like grain bins—cylindrical...exactly the shape...remembering those one passed driving out over the rutted roads. The same routes she often dreamed of as passages to better things. Such as a lime laden or elm heavy driveway poised within a privacy, a refinement, a collection of tested images with their fragrances not here in the grain struck air, the summits of flour rising like pillows over the landscape. And her imagination hastened to where all was still, aged, and quartered.

The curl papers were shredded, dropped onto the floor, parquet as she had wished, yet so disturbed by its removal here to Minneapolis, broken in spots and mended that the surface reflected a suffering which she shared and thus its beauty (like hers) did little to comfort her. She tore into the curl papers as she would attack a silo, knowing she had rendered them useless as the silo wrestled from its usefulness would in turn relinquish the fortune that yet sustained her.

There was a poem with
A Moon in it travelling across the bridge in one
Of those fragile trains carrying very small loads
Like moons that one could never locate anywhere else.
The Mississippi was bright under the bridge like a
Sun, because the poem called itself the Sun also;
Two boxcars on the bridge crossing the river.

June

dust dust dust dust dust dust
only small rain small rain small
thin thin rain starved rain rin

THE TÜRLER LOSSES

Türler patterns
    distinct as
    Palmyra ruins

Nighthawk

Peen   t   Pee n t
the shriek tenses when that shadow passes
"and midnight all a glimmer"

The crossed panes keep the shadow
peent is heard
in scraps   against   dawn
listen
                    wind scraps
grass ashiver
            field   tree   profile
                        Peen   t
take oath upon't
                    Nighthawk gothic

The sun dropped its leaf like a sun diary
turning a page to shadow where the body lay
in the shrubbery. The body moved, but with a stilly
motion the way a wave curls over a birthday
where nothing remains except the foam streamers,
like giggles after deep laughter, like death closing in.
It should be falling, no tears. It isn't. Mournful?
Yes, the sand's ribbon overturning the shell. The mollusc
pause. Such prettiness the shell and drip of water,
later dryness lent to a shelf.

The body no longer moved. That body is a bird
without rhythm or tied to decanters.
making informal wind notations, then love.

Wrist watches surround themselves with danger.
Signs. Worn clasps. Their time flies, stops.
Gallops. On a street. Dropped like an egg from a tree.
Expensive signals flashed in moonlight. Semi serious
stones wearing themselves out on wrists reaching
for decanters.

I like innocuous rhythms, don't you?
Less isn't so important.
When nothing lies there wearing a ring,
even the Türler loses time.

Water's blue day in the pool
the lake beyond its rim, even that temple
quoting distance an hypothesis,
tricked by fog, three columns reduced to two.
Water's depth and splash
thought margins.

Today the children lived in syllables pushing rafts
pushing themselves, the clime of heads on them the sun—
balconies, a summer stroll to odalisques. Later
a strewn room, the actors gone, disappeared
the pottery flowers. Méchant.

I miss the sparrow heads. Heads dip into the pool
as that smaller mark of time the arrow on the Türler face.
Tone values important when pointing out the
landscape.

I'll take you back to the station. Later
there'll be time.

Butterflies are silly, "planes of illumination"

Substantial contents alert in tombs. Presences.
As loss is absence.

"skipping along the Roman road eating
a tomato…"

Encountering the marble exactitude of things.
The precise pared from the round, the nubile.
Dawn after nightfall fog…heavy semblance
sheltering like that chair. Waiting for balance.

Moving into elsewhere music moves us
to boulders.
These columns. Shadows secure in thunder.
As boats move thick against water, forests
contained by sky.
These are contents.
Loss gropes toward its vase. Etching the way.
Driving horses around the Etruscan rim.

After the second Türler loss
a lessening perhaps of fastidiousness
                the Timex phase
and who says the wind blows to hurricane
escaped virtue...or that indeed
Timex is ripeness
the scent of potato field

Time calls hoarsely for sorbets and gestures
of sparrow; when locked in rhyme the door
sways and whines like a thief,
"the thief of time" was the original fellow
pushed out there on the street, caught beneath a wave,
leaves brushing past and weed tumbled.
The wintry awful noises of sleep with empty
harkening, lids crossing cheeks like pines
swept outside the sun, glitter of parakeet
tickles the eve, an awakening from warmth,
breeze on the lamp and the ridge, something cold
like an ice counts the chimes.

Out of this the Türler face
throat against darkness, we say a nose
examines with dignity, gives thrust
the painter uses the nose like a trowel.
See there René Char!
Differs from the Goya nose Don Carlos
with a filigree of disaster.

The apparatus on knees, yes supplicating
behind the crystal, the olive light dims
as the ambulance beam brightens and the highway
sombre while time passes
like death on certain stars moments on the stairs
or twilight when sand darkens
the wave shaped like time at its lamppost
all shades drawn, the intact crystal

Pauses between apparatus and crystal.
Pauses examined like sand those areas
we examine while waiting.

"Time's fool."

        Vases! Throats! Lactations!
The milk of time in the reservoir moon
           Stones with cloud current as sylphs
in nightclothes swim, moon on thicket
stems climb vases, wastrels.

(I wondered if he had taken my poems away with him.
I could find no smell of it, the poem. I understood
the need to explore. Departure imminent. Landings made
every day. Fragile marks made firmer as the eyes adjust
to horizons. Perhaps even now the poems lay in his valise,
unpacked. Perhaps they were unwritten. The poems were
huddled somewhere. They might be picked over by now.
Tossed from bed to bed or hand to hand. Greasy, losing
the glossy surface. I still refused to believe they
would disappear like the Türler watches. He could not
be so careless as to drop a poem on the street, let it slip
from its black strap like a watch struggling, embittered,
neglected, slipped off the broken stem of a watch band.
I read the letter from a firm called "White Walls", the
revered immaculate surface on which words pleaded me to
place a photograph of my poem about a photograph or
leniently, if I wished, to send a poem pasted to a white
wall. I thought of the white poem I had written whose face
might even now be speckled with dust, and the white pen
used to which I attached the poem's name, "The White Pen".
Surely among the belongings in the kit where the shoe polish
was kept there might be my "White Pen" with cream in its
nostrils.)

More and more memory began to circumambulate the
Türler losses. It began with the arrival in Zurich.

Strained hotel morning. Enjoyment of balcony,
clouds. Descend to garden. Decision to take
trolley to grave of Joyce. Return by trolley.
Downhill trip by taxi to Zurich. Lengthy promenade
of Strasse. Decision to make first Türler timepiece
purchase.

(Will enact same motions for purchase of second watch,
deleting trip to graveyard. Insert instead taxi ride
to gallery. Lack money to pay taxi. Search for bank
which is located immediately thanks to monetary geography
of Zurich.)

Passage to hotel made difficult by rain, yet spot the
Nervenklinic.

A year later visit Strasse and buy second Türler
timepiece with further trip to railway station where
someone takes a train to a mountain. There is the
added vertigo enhanced by the Swiss currency exchange.

Little did I expect the following year to lose the
second watch at Lexington Avenue and Eighty-sixth
in Manhattan.

Nor did I foresee I would read the Zurich Journal by…

Hatching away in her nuttery, she came to a sign saying
FLING. Actually she was too troubled by heights to
throw herself over, but she did observe that tokens were
necessary, so she took off her old watch and FLUNG.
Immediately upon descending from the tower she ran into
difficulties in the person of Markie who asked her what
was missing from her wrist.

That evening when Junie brought in the shepherd's pie
there was more contretemps all agreeing that anyone
without a watch was unreliable, but that to lose a
watch was even more UNRELIABLE.

It was she who suffered the most. Alone on her ledge
there was no familiar tick-tock to comfort her. When
morning finally announced itself in the shape of over-
head spinning and clumping she resolved to go into
Zurich even if it meant encountering slipshod vowels all
the way.

The first part of the journey was free of hazard. Just
outside the city she met a kindly Zwinglian curate who,
taking his arm out of its sling, pointed in the direction
of his own watch and told her to bear slightly to the right.

The road branched and ricocheted. The noise of pebbles
pinched her ears. A small bird fell from its roost.
She could scarcely believe that these were the perils
of a city to whom exiles turned in despair and disgust.

Faithfully she pursued the curate's instruction and
in less time than it takes to read ENGLISCH SPOKEN
she had entered a shop where the second Türler watch
was purchased.

At home she recorded this event in her DIARY, JOURNAL,
LETTERS, and the Sundry Shopping Lists later discovered
nestling in the shrubbery outside her workroom.

Your loss softened by that golden
museum. By tales when sudden air pours
through the still castle. Birds sing difficult
songs no other birds can sing. The spindle
whirls and gossamer appears. Faces stare
in dark comers as from trundle beds we
converse in rhyme. Wishes newly pasted.

Soon the regular hours would be let in.

Though nothing can bring back the hour

What was the other look you brought?
Houses with gardens, laughter like
the necessary wreath?

Wearing your Timex you gathered the October harvest.

Every inch dowsed by rain
pumpkins rotting and corn,
no tassel there, no sheaves
coves windswept. That summery wristband
blue and yellow faded like folded skin
voices overheard pacing acres
in the archery mud.

"We've all got to take our lumps."

You made the autumn ginger cookies

Sniggered like mules, kind of a dumb show.

Let that embrace last on the rim of the inkstand.
Wearing a white collar and the weight of it
holds you down like glaze, like Zurich.

You are creating two watches.

You enter the laboratory. Look out for the watch
called "Never Loses."

*Wordsworth

(Later they embrace as winter slides over the sill.
outdoors we would wear snowcaps on our skulls.)

Don't interrupt.

Continued in the kitchen under the Seth Thomas.

Seemingly realistic codes have pointed to other levels of images beyond their limits, ice permitting time to decorate a block.

Likely rivers graduating into lakes the desolate curve
my image against your shoulder, the homespun
logic of our twosomeness, a fabric time
will displace the threads, a shrivel here,
there a stain, the rotting commences like lanes
of traffic hurtling into air as the sun comes down.

Subterfuge

When the tribal months
come trooping over the clocks

I'll have mine plain
or I'll wear the brown.

Another old magazine while something
darts into the shallows

Tensions as the clock strikes
muttering envelopes, envelopes
"clouds surround their faces."

Seeking the chute or drifting
these rafts hourless in the breathing
admire the quarter hour
brave sofas surround

Breathing test while we waltz
a curious toe pointed toward hours

Eyes with negative irises shutting
as the minutes fly
birds crossing the deep chambers

Shoes at the fireplace or homogeneity
decided while the drops
elaborated before our envious vision

A child entered the room
wearing a clock costume
A child of pigmy size
unmodified by time's blisters

And time's throat burrs and time's screens
across which time's numerals

Flash ruptures

Look now forwards and let the backwards be

1

Frost villages on the slope
that's the bell peal
icy mountain time!

Scampering to the inn carrying our pumpkins
best not to be late in this region
rites are observed
habits called "old as time itself"
women go coiffed.

2

Arriving at sea level he hands her a Valentine
named "Coast,"
the sky is white and grey like February
the waves whiter while reflecting the sky
in patches of thickness that beat
on the coast with timely strikes
preparing sand exits.
She holds this landscape
the wet snow falls over it.

*Ouspensky

3

There were movements
in the garden with leaves and bicycles

Torpors suffered under cellophane
ripening and grasping

4

A bride and groom wait
beneath a canvas, cellophane
separates them from elements,
the groom steals a look at his watch
he would like to ride off
into the far bicycle spring.

5

Autre temps, autre mœurs

Yes I'd like to reorganize
the way it was in the October scheme.

A wrist for every watch
releasing doves

In the blown haze
a search for crystal

Broken glass

from FAIR REALISM

The Farewell Stairway

after Balla

The women without hesitancy began to descend
leaving flowers—

Ceres harried—bragged of cultivated grain—

I saw Hecate. the gray-wrapped woman.
in lumpy dark.

farewell eyes revolve—
the frontier oscillating—

pleated moments.
Hades at the bottom—

*

they laughed like twins their arms around each other
the women descending—

birds dropping south out of wind.

I thought there were many. goodbyes twisted
upwards from the neck—

tiny Arachne donating a web—

*

a common cloudy scene. no furniture.
a polished stairwell—

women magnetized. moving. chatting.

responding to the pull—
the vortex—

*

curves rapidly oscillating—

undulating to rapid pencil lines.

or water—

the look of stewed water.
sensuously.

and gnarled Charon—

*

their clothes—volumes—

folded over. blowing.
dresses approach the wide pencilling—

Hecate was present
and that other woman looking backward—

tearful. holding onto the rail.

I saw it futurally—

stoppered cotton slowly expanding. released.
sliding from the bottle—

*

I was outside the vortex. close to the wall.
Hecate managed me—

at the curve. the magic.
floated up—spiralled—

*

they were fully dressed. their volume.
the modish descent—

antiqueness—

*

a roman *scala*.

in the neighborhood of the *stazione*.

gli addii—gli addii—
velocity—

whipped the waves.

the vortex centered. reverent.

*

you who are outside. over there.
can't feel the pull. it makes you wonder—

the oscillation. the whirling. urgent.
indicating air revolving in a circuit—

without interruption. free movement
in *cielo puro*—spider-less—

       scatters everything.

something overheard—beyond Lethe.
whispered—and the corollary—

       *

diminuendo on the stair.
the slowed *salutando*—
flagrant barking from the shore—

keeping a stylish grip on themselves. serapes.

       futurally extended.

       *

south dusk and fire balls—

the same at Nauplia. mythic potency—

winding down the tower—

farewell. farewells.

An Emphasis Falls On Reality

Cloud fields change into furniture
furniture metamorphizes into fields
an emphasis falls on reality.

"It snowed toward morning," a barcarole
the words stretched severely

silhouettes they arrived in trenchant cut
the face of lilies....

I was envious of fair realism.

I desired sunrise to revise itself
as apparition, majestic in evocativeness,
two fountains traced nearby on a lawn....

you recall treatments
of 'being' and 'nothingness'
illuminations apt
to appear from variable directions—
they are orderly as motors
floating on the waterway,

so silence is pictorial
when silence is real.

The wall is more real than shadow
or that letter composed of calligraphy
each vowel replaces a wall

a costume taken from space
donated by walls....

These metaphors may be apprehended after
they have brought their dogs and cats
born on roads near willows,

willows are not real trees
they entangle us in looseness,
the natural world spins in green.

A column chosen from distance
mounts into the sky while the font
is classical,

they will destroy the disturbed font
as it enters modernity and is rare....

The necessary idealizing of you reality
is part of the search, the journey
where two figures embrace

This house was drawn for them
it looks like a real house
perhaps they will move in today

into ephemeral dusk and
move out of that into night
selective night with trees,

The darkened copies of all trees.

The Thread

Welcome brutal possessor
of the memory cards,
on the wall under wainscoting
a nail holds the thread.

Allegories ranged invisibly
variances of touch
lapses in speech
the urn burial containing ashes
of belonging to lightning.

We have not taken heroines
to snow, thrust hair under waterfalls,
we sent them to museums
they own splendid eyelashes,
giantesses who wear no clothes.

Sharing mineral fasts
to extend our eyes vertically
we advance beyond
an expectation of number
in bodies that swim at the last moment.

This concern for time
exists in memory cold
it is innocent of earth that suggested you.

Heavy Violets

Heavy violets there is no way
if the door clicks the cushion
makes murmur noise and the woman
on the sofa turns half in half out
a tooth slipping from velvet.

The world makes this division
copied by words each with a leaf
attached to images it makes of this
half in air and half out
like haloes or wrists

That separate while they spin
airs or shadows if you wish,
once or twice half in half out
a real twirl jostles there
lips creased with violets you wish.

Dora Maar

1

A woman weeping about an imaginary fall from a bicycle
"the bicycle has been stolen", he knows
it waits outside her door, asleep
a piece of *tailleur* on the brake:—

"her hair was all disheveled and her clothes were torn"
enemies had grabbed the wheel, they upset her and threw
her to the ground, she said
she had a knob on her forehead from the fall—
when he places his hand there he finds nothing
only the shift of veins he once painted.

This girlishness should feed on mirrors,
if there had been a fairy tale…to influence
her noise about damnation and enemies,
mystical exhortations he dislikes—
she moved about the room so nervously,

She tells him to repent:
"you are a cactus of stars."

2

In a cafe he watched her throw the knife
between the fingers of a gloved hand—
her character pasted with drama,
lights of rhinestone green....

he is the collagist who admires the gloves and green....

3

At Antibes they stroll the narrow streets
watch the night fishing—
her noble forehead is a sand cap water deftly clears,
one of her eyes is red, the other blue like a portrait
of Marie-Thérèse though bolder
with brunette make-up similar to *a poem by Eluard*
where black runs out of color....

He sees her as *the woman who weeps,*
her tears benefit his painting—
when he made the bull
or a woman flinging her hand from a window
she was that woman holding a light

She was the woman who fell from the house
in the daylight bombing—

She photographed the hysterical success
stage by stage with her alphabet of sighs
without liveliness—
her tears damage the heirloom.

4

once he had drawn her torso with wings
afterwards she saw the river
with a translucent depth
when her arm was a wing....

she changed into the oryx he shadows.

5

Her appearance is meddled with like *Io*
the tears are mother-of-pearl—

Eclectic and careless like Jove when changed
into a bull he finds the classical
screams of maidens exciting....

He raids her hallucinatory bicycle for an object
he calls "found" as the handles and bicycle seat
are transformed—

Jovian in dispensation of property—

6

She was given a farmhouse filled with spiders
in a land of dried raisins—

The invisible occult is her halo and hangs over her
when she washes linen—as she tends the smudge pots
she is guarded—

Sweetness returns to her scorched tongue....

Once she had known people who enjoyed verbal pleasure
and employed long sentences to restore their grandeur,
or stanzas to refine the lyricism of their meandering—

These artisans are valued by the medieval stone in
the holy village where even a dove is made of stone

The old weights—sand, a limpid ceiling,
blunt charcoal lift

Grief is banished from her coveted roost.

The Screen of Distance

1

On a wall shadowed by lights from the distance
is the screen. Icons come to it dressed in capes
and their eyes reflect the journeys their nomadic
eyes reach from level earth. Narratives are in
the room where the screen waits suspended like
the frame of a girder the worker will place upon
an axis and thus make a frame which he fills with
a plot or a quarter inch of poetry to encourage
nature into his building and the tree leaning
against it, the tree casting language upon the screen.

2

The telephone is Flaubert's parrot and it flitters
from perch to perch across the city. Or someone
is holding the dead thing in her hand in a remote
hotel. A sensitive person with a disability who
speaks to the inanimate. She may even resemble
Louise Colet or the helpful niece. She hasn't sent
her meaning and I am absent in these reminiscences
of her. The telephone is the guignol of
messages.

It may have been cold moving down from roofs,
a continental wind caught between buildings.
Leaves and pollen blowing onto fire escapes.
Windstruck hambones lying in a gutter. Equinoc-
tial changes the body knows, the hand feels, the
truck passes without notice and buildings con-
tinue their nervous commitments. The earth may
have been moaning underneath this junk. I am
caught in the wind's draft.

3

At night viewing the screen of distance
with shadowy icons framed by light
I understood the rasping interior
was rearing other icons,

No longer gentle they flashed ripened clauses,
or images raised formidable projections of ice,
the wall was placed in a temporary position
where words glittered from a dark cover,

Narcissism lived in a silver hut.

4

In the lighter time of year words arrived
concealed in branches. Flaubert exchanged
himself for words, night became a night of
words and a journey a journey of words, and
so on.

Words became "a superior joke", I trembled
under a revolutionary weight, a coward fleeing
from a cloud. The ego of words stretched to
the room's borders assuming the sonorous
movement of a poem.

5

I entice this novice poem with a mineral, *Beryl*.
The dictionary bestows on Beryl a skittish description,

like a sequence in which a car
moves over ruptured roads and slices
into ghost veins of color—
a camera follows each turn,
examines the exits where rock protects
a visionary tool that prods it:—

"A light greenish blue that is bluer
and deeper than average aqua,
greener than robin's eggs blue,
bluer and paler than turquoise
blue and greener and deeper than beryl
blue—a light greenish blue that is bluer
and paler than beryl or average turquoise blue—
bluer and slightly paler than aqua."

The speculative use of mineral prevents an
attachment to words from overflowing, inserts
a vein of jazz, emblems of color and overcomes
the persecuting stretch of racetrack where words
race their mounts ....

6

Beryl became a distraction as one speaks of color
field or someone as a colorist or of color pre-
dominant, so the paper on which the poem would
rest was grainy with color flashing lights
and the depth, the deepness of the country lane
on which shadows found repose was a wilderness of
color, ditches and trees lost their contours. I
created a planned randomness in which color
behaved like a star.

7

To introduce color to form
I must darken the window where shrubs
grazed the delicate words
the room would behave
like everything else in nature,

Experience and emotion performed
as they did within the zone of distance
words ending in fluid passages
created a phenomenal blush
dispersing illusion ....

8

A difficult poem intrudes like hardware
decorating a quiet building, a tic taking
over the facade, a shrug exaggerated by a
column—

Shelley sailing into the loose wind,
the storm of neurosis hindering the formal plan,
a suggested dwelling left on the drawing board
with clumps of shrubs indicating hysteria or,

Daylight gleams on the rough street where a
blameless career sighs, the poet beak dips
in air, his little wings cause a mild stir,
as someone comes down the stair
he pleads with infancy,

A woman speaks to a dish, old forks, amid her
preparations she smiles touched by history.
Chipped, sundry evidences of temporal life
hiding in a bush. In formal dress domestic
remarks reel into a corpus known as stanzas.

9

The Bride raised the cloud settled on her
aspen head and stepping away from her bachelors
she seized like wands the poem I handed her:

"A life glitters under leaves
piled for anonymity…"

She would lead us through glass to view the
enigmatic hill where a castle slung a shadow.

10

There was a dream within a dream and inside
the outer dream lay a rounded piece of white
marble of perfect circular dimension.
The dreamer called this marble that resembled
a grain of Grecian marble, "Eva Knachte,"
who was blown into the dream by the considerate
rage of night.

Her name evoking night became a marble pebble,
the land on which she rested was the shore
of the sea that washed over her and changed
her lineaments into classic marble, a miniature
being, yet perfect in this dream, her size
determined by the summer storm with which
I struggled and seized the marble.

The marble was a relic, as were the movements
of nature on the poem. The sea had lent
a frieze, waves a shoulder when the investitures
of a symbolic life feuded. In that dimness
with bristles, straw, armor plate, grotty
Alexandrines there appeared a mobile fiction ....

11

A man who calls himself a Baron yet strays from
his estate into the cadmium yellow
of a bewildering sunset rendered by apprehension
where a broad approach to a narrow tunnel
is fanned by leaves is faced with a decision——
at the stylized ominous entrance he wonders
if reality will maintain him or empathic snow
subdue his quest....

12

I sifted through these fictive ambiguities
until there was a plain moment
something like a black table where

Dialogue set in motion urged a search
in memory for that tonal light
illuminating the screen,

The Baron faded as distance gleamed
a clear jar multiplied by frost.

Wild Gardens Overlooked by Night Lights

Wild gardens overlooked by night lights. Parking
lot trucks overlooked by night lights. Buildings
with their escapes overlooked by lights

They urge me to seek here on the heights
amid the electrical lighting that self who exists,
who witnesses light and fears its expunging,

I take from my wall the landscape with its water
of blue color, its gentle expression of rose,
pink, the sunset reaches outward in strokes as the west wind
rises, the sun sinks and color flees into the delicate
skies it inherited,
I place there a scene from "The Tale of the Genji."

An episode where Genji recognizes his son.
Each turns his face away from so much emotion,
so that the picture is one of profiles floating
elsewhere from their permanence,
a line of green displaces these relatives,
black also intervenes at correct distances,
the shapes of the hair are black.

Black describes the feeling,
is recognized as remorse, sadness,

black is a headdress while lines slant swiftly,
the space is slanted vertically with its graduating
need for movement,

Thus the grip of realism has found
a picture chosen to cover the space
occupied by another picture
establishing a flexibility so we are not immobile
like a car that spends its night
outside a window, but mobile like a spirit.

I float over this dwelling, and when I choose
enter it. I have an ethnological interest
in this building, because I inhabit it
and upon me has been bestowed the decision of changing
an abstract picture of light into a ghost-like story
of a prince whose principality I now share,
into whose confidence I have wandered.

Screens were selected to prevent this intrusion
of exacting light and add a chiaroscuro,
so that Genji may turn his face from his son,
from recognition which here is painful,
and he allows himself to be positioned on a screen,
this prince as noble as ever,
songs from the haunted distance
presenting themselves in silks.

The light of fiction and light of surface
sink into vision whose illumination
exacts its shades,

The Genji when they arose
strolled outside reality
their screen dismantled,
upon that modern wondering space
flash lights from the wild gardens.

Words

The simple contact with a wooden spoon and the word
recovered itself, began to spread as grass, forced
as it lay sprawling to consider the monument where
patience looked at grief, where warfare ceased
eyes curled outside themes to search the paper
now gleaming and potent, wise and resilient, word
entered its continent eager to find another as
capable as a thorn. The nearest possession would
house them both, they being then two might glide
into this house and presently create a rather larger
mansion filled with spoons and condiments, gracious
as a newly laid table where related objects might gather
to enjoy the interplay of gravity upon facetious hints,
the chocolate dish presuming an endowment, the ladle
of galactic rhythm primed as a relish dish, curved
knives, finger bowls, morsel carriages words might
choose and savor before swallowing so much was the
sumptuousness and substance of a rented house where words
placed dressing gowns as rosemary entered their scent
percipient as elder branches in the night where words
gathered, warped, then straightened, marking new wands.

The Nude

Studios are stations of reminiscence
in the nimble wind they are shadows

The artist attaches himself to the shadow
he attempts to revive it after the wind ceases,

This mixture of dark and light
is mysterious and adds depth

To the position of his model
who rephrases the shadow.

She reminds him of attitudes
beyond the mere appraisal of subject,

A peace without clothes
with its bestowal of light and volume

Where nudism is born.

The behavior of the landscape of nudism
varies as mirrors reflect

Curves, syllables of grace,
drops of water or trees elastic,

A native body beneath its plumes.

Is a weight become effervescent
when attacked by knowledge

Of shells and other remainders
of sexual consciousness tossed from sand,

They live in a contradiction of time.

The narcissism of the artist escapes into a body
that defines his emotions,

An interior where his own contour is less misty.

The figure is a nominal reminder that existence
is not pantomime as relieved by the artist,

The body of the model, the lift of her torso
the extension of limbs, fold of skin

Express reality beyond tenure of the brush,
shell or escapist sail,

A severe distance is established between her realism
and his anxious attempt to define it.

The painter desires the image he has selected
to be clothed in the absolute silk of his touch,

Lonely himself he has admired the glance
of kimonos, mirrors, fans and bestowed them on her

Who for many minutes of this day
borrows from art to cover her nudity.

The artist chose these objects to enrich space
around his model's hair or even her breathing

Which you notice as it shifts the atmosphere
in which you keep watch with a calm become necessary,

You are the viewer and without you
the picture cannot exist, the model shall cease to breathe.

The artist will sorrow even as darkness
replaces his brilliance of color

The viewer inherits this nude
as a reminder of his own weightlessness

In a natural world
made winsome, or tense or aggravated

By the requests of an unclad body
with its announcement of dimension and clarity.

The need of the artist to draw the body
is like the love for three oranges,

He searches the world to find those spheres
that will confine the fluid nude,

There is with him a desire elemental
in its urgency to savor the skin of the body

The hues of geranium before they exit
his allotment of reality.

As the swan entered Leda
so the actual timing of an artist's abrupt gesture

Is supernatural despite interferences
of local ornamental mundaneity,

The supernatural contacts ecstasy hidden
in a guise of nudism.

The artist borrows mannerisms and technique,
he is free to copy, the other world is ambitionless.

An aura once restless now subsists
through residual favors on reverence,

Eve stands by her cypress,
a quiet nude studied by Cranach,

The solid body is led through crocuses.

You are with an artist who notices everything
which concerns color and shape.

In the restaurant the artist says a blouse
you are wearing goes with the decor.

The blouse is a watery blue like somewhere
off the coast of Greece, like these walls

The colors you wear tumble into mild earth tones
again like a country, nothing literary

Where the rough body reaches out
a wave rushes over the sand denuding it

You share the classical nude landscape of sand.

At times a silence overcomes the artist,
a fog at the base of columns,

He explains he is thinking of the body.

Its behavior is strange, hiding behind leaves
he can never trap or bribe it.

So deep is the body's memory of self.

Each day there is a different voice,
today while wearing no clothes

It spoke of the essentials of life which were evident,
but the body took an invisible position,

It is arguable whether he shall ever see the face,
her back was turned from him like a goddess

She was either admiring herself or bathing.

Morning traverses her breasts
where she sits under the window of white curtains,

Trees are outside, their branches fix the sky,
she is thinking of nudism,

He draws an odalisque,
it is love they are asking for.

She looks at a canvas,
nature covets it,

Where a fever blots the muslin
clouds start to rise.

There is no figure.

This is landscape,
portrait of nude melancholy

Or its glow which is austere,
she asks, where am I?

He has not drawn her,
the sheen of her body only survives.

She turns herself into a star
above the unattended foliage,

He views her as she glistens,
silver enters the picture.

He confides,
"Each day I define myself."

He notices a coarseness of flesh,
he thickens his paint,

"It is a glimpse into the future,
fields light up," she sighs.

To replenish the sallow on her throat
he adds sunset tint

She reaches for ombre, noir
"It is the narrowness of time."

Respectful moonlight inhabits them.

from DEFENSIVE RAPTURE

Paulownia

I

ravenous the still dark a fishnet—
  robber walk near formidable plaits
  a glaze—the domino overcast—

seized by capes—budding splash
whitened—with strokes—
   silvertone gravure.
    knifed tree.

straw beneficence—
      ambient cloud. riderless.

II

vowels inclement—tossed off figure
  lisping blot—
    running fiigure.
    bowled ripe.
stood in the wind sheet. a fermur axis.
  virginal wail. as grain. storm motif.

III

pierced the risen sea.
        coxcomb.
slides around.

        day and night.

        "remedy of darkness"
            lit body.

IV

etched in powder

sequence—a solace

        the monument.
        width of grape—is praised.

V

        adherence to sand
the loam division—the quagmire

            foot sink the rind—
        or   rindswift heel
astonished acre
                chewed wire.

VI

as instrument

threaded sky
burnt.
torn from the corner.
on your knees

VII

plinth in sour bloom.

the idiot cone. rummage.

VIII

held   in mortar air.

'weight of stone'

fragment.

IX

their whole selves—
or were they?

burden of face
from one to the other

quaking sun.

abstract arm.

The Surface as Object

the visible

as in the past

subsisting in layered zone

refuses to dangle

oaths on marsh field

whitened or planned

memorial distance

rather than vine

that which proliferates

the bittersweet grapple

initiates

a mysterious mesh

forbids   the instant disclosure

delays a humid course

or creates a patina

jungleware.

or she moving forward into

the line of sticks

circled by sticks

her hand flies up

in the direct line of sticks

odor of lines.

knowing the difficulty

annexation of Egypt

oaths on marsh fields etc.

a possible intimacy with

the tomblike fragrance of stone

the cult-like

expressiveness.

(the perpendicular

millimeter stone

less raw

or, gangling

as the artful

lessening surprised.)

tree grown guava

oaths on marsh field

the hungry minstrel and the forager

gold on the guava lick of rosin

and the chill latched thicket

marsh weed

regardez-la

the untamed ibis.

Defensive Rapture

Width of a cube spans defensive rapture
cube from blocks of liquid theme
phantom of lily stark
in running rooms.

adoration of hut performs a clear function
allusive column extending dust
protective screen the red
objects pavilion.

deep layered in tradition moonlight
folkloric pleads the rakish
sooted idiom
supernatural diadem.

stilled grain of equinox
turbulence the domicile
host robed arm white
crackled motives.

sensitive timbre with complex
astral sign open tent hermetic
toss of sand swan reeds
torrents of uneveness.

surround a lusted fabric
hut sequence modal shy
as verdigris hallow force
massive intimacy.

slant fuse the wived
mosaic a chamber astrakhan
amorous welding
the sober descant.

turns in the mind bathes
the rapture bone a guardian
ploy indolent lighted
strew of doubt.

commends internal habitude
bush the roof
day stare gliding
double measures.

qualms the weights of night
medusæ raft clothed sky
radiant strike the oars
skim cirrus.

evolve a fable husk
aged silkiness the roan
planet mowed like ears
beaded grip.

suppose the hooded grass
numb moat alum trench a solemn
glaze the sexual estuary
floats an edge.

Restlessness

1

oh conscript not the forest
a stone and laughter

it sports a halo
filled with drops one after the other

in the efficacious zone they fall like minerals

and the courtesans move to a narrow spot
where their lids are tinted and the slight
huskiness of

a cat's mouth enters.

2

*it was when I stayed with her that I first heard the sound of
violin and piano and orchestra...*

in that part of the forest these instruments were unknown
...the first 'scent' of the West.

3

he swims holding the wood handle
eyes smudged below the iris
burned leaves thrown from her fingers

wildlife running from the edge
four persons inside a hut
a passage from the shared bowl
throwing the rind outside the bowl.

grown ups working in the forest
tidying hair at the car window
noodles, plasticity.

4

now they move through indigo
the shape of their shoulder
armpit
even the bag of garnets
they rave about steals from
dark blue and they
wish to copulate
in that medium
hands in the noodles

wayfare in shadow city.

5

a lantern
among the grasses
    smoke from white lanterns;

yonder the corpse
wrapped in straw.

insect voices
    filtering through the woodcut

upon the tombstone the last
poem of *Takahashi O-den*

    oh the straw hunchedness.

6

even the willow
vanished from Tama River

the shivering flavor
disappeared.

naphtha on her skin.

when he stays with her
'the violins the piano and orchestra'

the western 'scent.'

---

italics on page 163: Hasegawa Shigure

Borderlands

The return was like a snowbird like the cutoff

before the orchard we remembered;

they came to us as rustlers

the steeds were foam.

The girl in the bonnet the man with shoulder pads

were familiar the rustic was anyone's choice

he chortled; there was mutual glee

it clammered.

Welcome in a new fashion a century had passed

bones tucked away even wreaths

headbands

where orchards joined an isthmus was winter.

Our preoccupation began with grass hoeing when

    it starts to roam, folding down corners

watching the tubular form;

        desiring no money we were

serene like a nation.

       We shifted our feet, tribal

   at desolate speech or,

     canoeing a worn river,

fought separately when they held us up;

why is this remembered, how is it explained?

     "Escape with me!"

we hear them say and look at the drivelling

margin at the inch where stone refused to burn

    light on rural habitation.

You cannot tell them what glass resembles they

skid on the track;

reindeer eat moss

the subject is not the assassin.

Lands incorporated by the Treaty of Versailles in 1919 to form
Czechoslovakia: Bohemia, Moravia, Silesia, Slovakia, Ruthenia.

Dissonance Royal Traveller

sound opens sound

shank of globe   strings floating out

something like images are here

opening up avenues to view a dome

a distant clang reaches the edifice.

*

understanding what it means
to understand music

cloudless movement   beyond the neck's reach

an hypnotic lull in porcelain water break mimics

tonality crunch of sand under waddling

a small seizure
from monumentality

does not come or go   with understanding

the path will end

birdhouse   of trembling cotton

or dream   expelled it

parcel   on the landlocked moor.

*

explaining music

and their clothes entangled

who walk into a puddle of minnows;

minnows in a bowl

consonant with water.

the drifted footpad

ambushed by reeds signals the listening

oars.

music disappears into oars.

*

in the middle the world is brown;

on the opposite side of the earth

an aroma of scarlet.

this accompanies our hearing music;

the sleeve of heaven

and the hoof of earth

loosed from their garrison.

dissonance may abandon *miserere*

on bruised knee hasten to the idol.

*

and what is consonance—the recluse—

entering and exiting

as often as a monarch butterfly

touches a season;

by accident grips the burning flowers.

in the stops between terror

the moon aflame on its plaza.

*

autumn of rippling wind

and the noise of baskets

smell of tin fists.

and harsh fists

on the waterfall changing the season;

the horse romps in flax

a cardboard feature

creating a cycle of flax.

music imagines this cardboard

the horse in cardboard jacket

flagrant the ragged grove

red summit red.

dissonance royal traveller

altered the red saddle.

The Advance of the Grizzly

go from the must-laden room

move to the interior

the remarkable bird in the case;

    wing

(like a pillow).

bird out of cloud—dissembling of trees; locks;

the icicle; out of the margin

falling from the grim margin the axle of skin;

enamoured with the fell wing.

I will move in my skin with the hollow

the neck and the brimming over the latitude

over the latitude onto the brink.

frame of snow "within

squares of diminishing size"

ink hushed the snow; a blank sky rolled to the verge

parable heaved through drift...

and the moon weighted

with this the coil

evoked our willing to believe in a sudden pull

of the immense frame at the heel:

     spilled exactly

to destroy a circular return

from the ragged prose clump

clump on the cold landscape

white grown fatter... place of sharpened skin.

romantic fever and snow

fresh from the gorgon bed

dendrophagous "feeding on trees"

to sustain the romantic vision route over snow

the sudden drop into pines:

"feeding on trees"

new mouths red of Okeechobee.

(and ate the alligator and spat out the part

wedded to the green clavicle.)

loss of the sun

blight of the sun the looney forest

who will walk out of the plush interior into

the excited atmosphere?

an outlet for prose the advance of the grizzly.

The Glass Mountain

in memory of J.S.

I

king as wanderer

replied   we do and always

the least recounting

pelting dew

bird in the sunrise room;

once or twice the landscape burns

what we are after tires

clouds mohair.

rhododendron bring

     pods to the mountain;

a tremulous position

harp on a mountain of glass.

II

is it a power

you pass in the night

taking water from the tap,

fog or phantom

the king stares at.

you are not the snake lady

gold filament above

the snake limbs

nor does she tell

who taught the dance.

III

the king watched

in flat country the

caravan at ewe season

a density

sand and thyme

near the threshold

where they milk

have bitten the nut-

like substance

IV

bauble of sound

mahogany the king

travelling the length

overhead a climate

of twang the rushed snow

unstoppable space in the bold

different in the next imagined

movement the breach

is inimitable

a phrase others believe

there is no escape

the towed rock dims.

v

why not live

image strewn

and goes pitter pat

next to the resolute corridor

and a diadem would hang on the fringe

actual pieces of tame fibre shut off.

on the steeple with the watercan

and thunder in the earring she

caught the speech of the termagant

the roll

was seen the plummage and owl

a raft on the cold river; skin

on the raft a king

picked up boards and sunk them.

VI

the shades lavished

in the ideal

climate of planets fear

steam rolling up;

holding hands in a ring

wet to their waists

        hair

a slippery blossom.

exposure beneath the May apse

        doggerel;

chunks of filched

    objects not

lapidary; a king.

VII

attent on detail

    the hullabaloo over

rule half water half worn

    running the notion of land;

tells us where light comes from

    white curtains in its beak;

closer closer to the splintered mountain

O king endlessly

scattering.

Otranto

At sunset from the top of the stair watching

the castle mallets wrenched from their socket

fell from ambush into flame flew into hiding;

above the stoneware a latch like muscle hid

the green; he stood waist high under the rapt

ceiling and hanged the sparrow; where the kitchen

had been a mirror of eggs served in a tumbler he

saw the ring when a lancet pierced and threw it.

In a basket and lowered it where sails enter

the harbor over a parchment like dominoes;

the petrel-like eyelash.

To the sun and its rites were pulled the dried

banners; they flew past the ruins the tower

and window where ivory guided the mist on his back;

he rubbed his eyes and counted them kneeling

wrinkled as grass.

A ghost in their nostrils put a heel at their

forehead; they saw only the moon as it

fasted.

II

If the ship meant anything if he heard a world

view in the midst of his rhythm or the spell

lustrous like hair on his arm; that groaned as

it struck near the tumble down or

combing hair; words burnt as they quickened.

The bitter they share crept into forage and

muster is in their skin; the grey

worked like a vise they brushed this

to turn arrows; they shut off the vast

cellar and the turret leaped to a pattern;

the mosaic blended was untouched.

III

The frankish hills and hummocks metered

the greed over sun and cloud; voluptuous

in the straits turbanned held scarves to the

water each sail embroidered;

who washed in their music a lattice.

A major or borrowed sky this aspect provides

the lily stalk inside the frame; a gesture the lily

pointing north as if the wrench from sky decides

cold rain or change of tide; the lily

she chooses.

IV

Waking in must the high pierced window dew on

the furnaced bar the poaching hour the cup

takes smoke from the tower; they drink

in the smoke the print cradled; cut in dark.

The siege made cloth a transfer

learned from invaders who craved it;

spindle thieves.

She sang high notes and pebbles went into her

work where it changed into marks; in that room

the armor-like wrens:

rites turned with thread a dower

begs lapis; eglantine on a spoon; the castle

breeds tallow.

V

A change of tide might delay the run

they watched as if by simple water;

read magisterially whatever the book decided;

night outside covered with filmic screen

ghosts they store; then bring an experimental

wheel out of hiding.

Even the Nile wind; fortune cards

jugglers a remedy from old clothes;

to appease the fable—pearls

rolling in straw.

The way a cowslip bends

they remember or Troilus as he stared;

they agree on brighter covers; looser

shifts fluent tower to tower.

More ephemeral than roundness or

the grown pear tree connected

with vision a rose briar.

VI

There was only a rugged footpath

above the indifferent straits and a shelf where the

castle lay perhaps it was sphered like Otranto;

there the traveller stood naked and talked

aloud or found a lily and thought a sword;

or dragged a carcass upon blunt stone like a

corded animal. In weeds in spiritual

seclusion a felt hand lifted.

Winter Horses

placed two sticks upon a dazzling plate

unlike feudal wars you remember

their saying she is stalking

and the fortifications are blocked

abruptly they held their breath until it froze.

carpeting the greensward a foil of sunset

"idyll of the kings" and shut the moat;

did not forget the promised tawny

situation of splendor.

again twists in the passage

or is it rhythm overturned;

to regard moodily a cask something

borrowed or fable stuck the snow.

II

sea grey cold a door one boulder

slams another.

instantly footprints

in the sand corner.

grief spell was thought something else

records what was cried out.

the shrived warm

turns into serpent

are

no kingdoms

is grass.

III

winter

you know how it is *la gloire!*

they bring you a fig dish.

the dead in white cotton.

fleece on the platter.

wind crept

the white shoat and buried;

the cramped space ran

out of breathing.

IV

bars of snow lanced the brightness

crippled windows flung

lute with two notes unevenly.

ice breaking and noise

envelops sobriety.

slice of boot on the frayed sylph

came out of dazzlement into

fisheries was intended.

Chalk

I

you await assumptions induced by temperament—

ecclesiastic in wing power—

narrow abridgement   yellow slanders the island

lavable breeze work.

the catalogue within the visor—

reticule of mannerists.   employable objects.

minor tenses born in the scrubs—

irregular

flame—

exiled   grass.

II

voiceless Etruria

the mythic quarry—

fireball tunneled.

jovial stone   cipherless—

hijacked. lively.

III

with eyecatch—

on rocks off Scylla

silvered goats entering. leaving.

Memory plunge. tossed. refined.

post-attic rhythms juggled.

in beggar garb Odysseus

—the Cyclops pinched like rose plums.

'steals   memory'

brittle nosed.

shuttle loom.

IV

1

unfashionable—

bent at the waist. professional at descendant hour—

vase galop

unarmored amid

glued piecework   impotent   vessel—

Thracian meld.

skidded root power.

2

a fairly simple footwork

the body painted white—

an air of decay   in the toothless pattern

light in controlled areas—lavender extensions—

the chambers tied into bundles

says the body.

an oiled leap

embracing the skin   minimal in shyness

circling—crumpling—rising

the six scenes.

cricket music for the robing.

v

the Orphic rite film releases

bathybius

miniature displacement. mountain   dialect partial.

(ph formally silent)

indices proper to songster.

zephyrstorm and flute—

heroic spin beneath subsoil—

regal smiles.   conversation shaded—

black currant tin.

VI

a half root elasticized

the upright valve a harpsichord

in steel diminuendo   *historicism—*

alabaster hooded—

reduces complex Medea—the narrow unbridled hand—:

"mere   antique queen"

aisle of lopped off heads

VII

little is missing even plumped shadow—

a knight observes his dress—

under the rough mountain

tree growth out of rock.

a natural tone in the poems.

lid pried open   volumes fall out—

lightning sinks into soft thunder and

weights of earth balance.

VIII

a slice paradisical

flickers into melted *jaune*

astrew the careless Arcadian—

red-tiled slumber. dowerless.

the waxed emptiness—moulting stone—

agrarian fable.

BARBARA GUEST

Winner of the Lawrence J. Lipton Prize (*Fair Realism*) and the San Francisco State Poetry Award (*Defensive Rapture*), Barbara Guest has come to receive the recognition she deserves. A festschrift celebrating her writing was hosted recently by Brown University. For those acquainted with contemporary poetry, Guest is an outstanding figure.

Born in North Carolina in 1920, Barbara Guest spent her childhood in Florida and California. After graduating from the University of California at Berkeley, she settled in New York City where she connected with the equally emerging New York Poets and artists of Abstract-Expressionism who were then to influence her poetry.

During the 1960s *The Location of Things, Poems,* and *The Blue Stairs* were published. *Moscow Mansions* (1973), *The Countess from Minneapolis* (1976), and in particular her novel *Seeking Air* (1978), pointed to a sense of structure moving in more varied and experimental directions. This was true of her acclaimed biography of the poet H.D., *Herself Defined* (1984), which had consumed five years, and especially of a major poem, *The Türler Losses* (1979), and of *Biography* (1980).

Fair Realism (1989) was followed by *Defensive Rapture* (1993), of which a critic has observed that Guest was now "pushing the reader into the spiritual and metaphysical possibilities of language itself."

Containing all of Guest's major poems and revealing lesser-known gems, *Selected Poems* is one of the major literary events of the decade.

The text of this book is set in *Aldus,* a crisply drawn 'old-style' face designed by the prolific Herman Zapf in 1953–54. Named for Aldus Manutius, master printer and publisher of the fifteenth century, Zapf's *Aldus* is modeled on the classic lines and proportions of the scribal letter of the Italian Renaissance.

Section titles are set in *Michelangelo,* also drawn by Herman Zapf in 1950 as a titling companion for his *Palatino,* while poem titles are set in *Diotima* italic with *Ariadne* initials. The latter faces were drawn in 1953–54 by Zapf's wife, Gudrun Zapf-Von Hesse.

Typeset by Guy Bennett.

*　*

*